P9-DMD-501

## DATE DUE

| | | |
|---|---|---|
| FEB 0 8 2002 | | |
| MAY -5 2004 | | |
| MAY -5 2004 | | |
| | | |
| | | |
| | | |
| | | |
| | | |
| | | |
| | | |
| | | |
| | | |
| | | |
| | | |
| | | |

DEMCO 38-297

# RISKY BUSINESS

# Window Washer

## At Work Above the Clouds

By

KEITH ELLIOT GREENBERG

*With Photography by Bob Strong*

A BLACKBIRCH PRESS BOOK

WOODBRIDGE, CONNECTICUT

Published by Blackbirch Press, Inc.
One Bradley Road
Woodbridge, CT 06525

©1995 Blackbirch Press, Inc.
First Edition

Printed in Hong Kong

10 9 8 7 6 5 4 3 2 1

**Special Thanks**
The author wishes to thank Theresa Affuso of the Port Authority
of New York and New Jersey—operators of the World Trade
Center—for her assistance in preparing this book.

**Additional Photo Credits**
Pages 12-13: ©Bruce Glassman/Blackbirch Press, Inc.; page 17:
©Bruce Glassman/Blackbirch Press, Inc.

**Library of Congress Cataloging-in-Publication Data**

Greenberg, Keith Elliot.
    Window washer/by Keith Greenberg.
      p.   cm. — (Risky business)
    Includes bibliographical reference and index.
    Summary: Profiles the life and work of Roko Camaj, a professional
window washer who cleans the windows on the observation tower of the
World Trade Center, the second tallest building in the world.
    ISBN 1-56711-154-8
    1. Window cleaners—United States—Juvenile literature. 2. Camaj,
Roko—Juvenile literature. [1. Camaj, Roko. 2. Window cleaners.]
I. Title. II. Series: Risky business (Woodbridge, Conn.)
HD8039.W492U64   1995
648'.5—dc20                                              94-41701
                                                              CIP
                                                              AC

# I N T R O D U C T I O N

The crowd on the Observation Deck of the World Trade Center is grateful for the clear sky on the other side of the large glass windows. It is a perfect day to view the sights from 107 stories above the busy streets of New York. Some look down on the Empire State Building and the Chrysler Building to the north. Others look at the Hudson River to the west and the famous Statue of Liberty to the south. All are enjoying the special view from the second-tallest building in the world.

Suddenly, the spectators are jolted by a surprising sight. Fifty-three-year-old Roko Camaj has popped into view on the outside of one of the windows! Unaware of the excitement inside, he continues scraping his squeegee across the glass. It is a curious way to make a living, but Roko loves it. When he isn't concentrating on shining the huge tower's windows, he's peeking down at the tops of clouds.

**Roko works on the outside of the World Trade Center, high above New York City.**

**People who see Roko hanging outside think he must be crazy to do his job.**

Several observers inside believe Roko is insane. Nobody normal would wash windows at such a height, they say. Some visitors try to show their thoughts to the man hanging outside the tower. A few point at the side of their head and roll their finger around and around.

Roko finds the whole thing funny. "I'm not crazy!" he shouts from his spot in the sky. Roko truly believes that he and his fellow window washers are no different than any other workers. "You don't have to be nuts to do this," he says. "The only thing is you shouldn't be scared of heights."

Roko often talks with visitors while he's outside.

7

**Roko arrives for work early each morning.**

Regardless of the weather, Roko follows a similar routine every day. He leaves his home at 5 AM, and takes the train into the city. Then, he transfers to a subway train. By 6 AM, he's at the World Trade Center.

On February 26, 1993, a terrorist bomb rocked the twin towers. Ever since then, security at the World Trade Center has been increased. Roko must sign his name to enter sections of the complex. Certain doors won't open for him unless he runs a computer-coded card through a scanner. Roko must even use his special card to ride the elevator that takes him up and down.

**For security reasons, World Trade Center employees must use a special card to move about the building.**

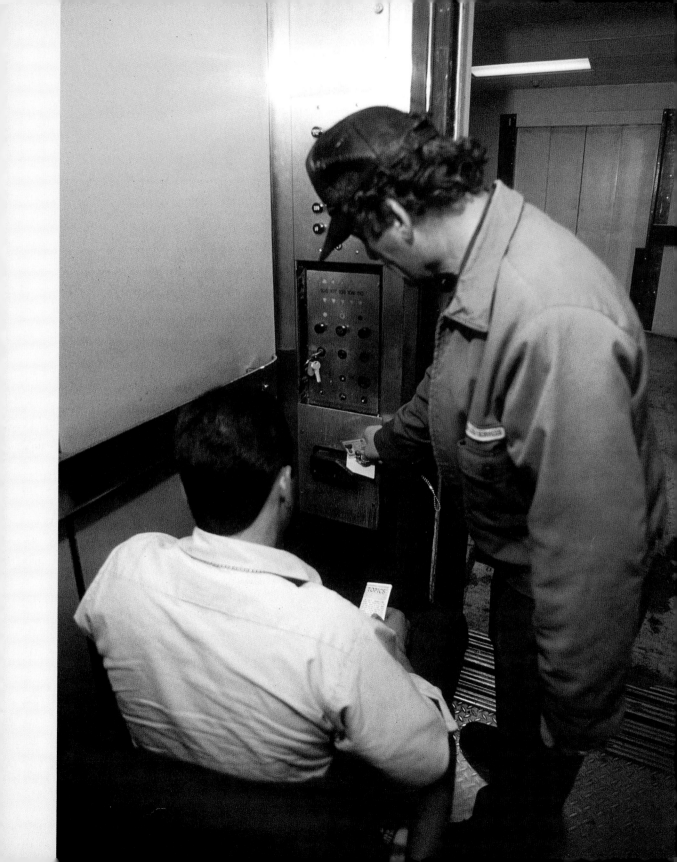

Roko makes his way to the top of the tower to meet his partner, James Meehan. Together, James and Roko work on a special rig, suspended thousands of feet in the air. Also on the roof is a 360-foot antenna that transmits television and radio signals.

A giant antenna on the roof sends radio and television signals.

In many ways, Roko's job is very pleasant.  When he starts his day— above the 110th floor of the 1,370-foot building—it is often clear enough to see five states:  New York, New Jersey, Connecticut, Pennsylvania, and Delaware.  With 600,000 square feet of glass to polish, Roko is proud of his role in making one of New York's famous landmarks sparkle.

**On a clear day, Roko can see five states from the roof.**

11

New York City seems small from so high up.

12

On the ground, New York is a noisy, busy town. But the atmosphere is peaceful from where Roko stands. Helicopters passing the building are far enough below him to look like toys. The city's mighty skyscrapers seem tiny. And the yellow taxi cabs from this height seem to slide along the streets below.

Once, a strong wind swept Roko's baseball cap off his head. He watched the hat fly over the neighboring World Trade tower, then disappear into the heavens. "It probably ended up in Canada," he chuckles.

As Roko grew up in Yugoslavia, he decided he wanted to live in a country with more freedom, where he could speak his mind.

"I always heard about America," he says. "People told me, 'If you move there, you will have a beautiful car and a big house. And there is freedom.' I thought it would be nice to go to a place where I could say whatever I wanted."

On August 17, 1969, Roko and his wife Katrina moved to New York. The very next day, their daughter Angelina was born. Roko couldn't speak English yet. But he knew that he needed a job—any job—to support his family.

**Roko's job has helped him become successful in America.**

15

In 1973, the World Trade Center was dedicated in a ceremony that drew interest around the world. At the time, the twin towers were the tallest structures in the world. (Only Chicago's Sears Tower would surpass them when it was completed in 1973). The World Trade Center was to be the capital of business activity in the Northeast. More than 350 firms set up offices in the complex. Every day, 50,000 people went to work at the many companies that deal in international banking, finance, transportation, insurance, and many other professions. Some 70,000 people visited the center each day.

**The World Trade Towers mark an important business center for the Northeast.**

16

After four years as a window washer at John F. Kennedy Airport in New York, Roko took a position washing some of the World Trade Center's 43,600 windows. "The first day, I was really nervous," he recalls. "I thought about getting stuck and hanging over New York."

Roko went to the top of the building and climbed into the special window-washing "basket" that travels up and down the tower. Suddenly, he felt cheerful about having a job at the World Trade Center. Over the coming weeks, he decided that he loved going to work.

"It's just me and the sky. I don't bother anybody and nobody bothers me," he says happily.

The window-washing basket surrounds workers up to the waist and makes them secure.

Roko checks the underside of the
window-washing machine.

Thanks to new technology, Roko and the other window washers don't have to do all the work by themselves. A window-washing machine can do much of the job. Circulating water and wiping off fluid with rotating squeegees and brushes, the machine glides up and down the first 100 stories. Because the liquid is being recycled as the machine cleans, a 20-gallon tank of water is good for 1,100 windows. It takes 20 minutes for the machine to go down the building. Then it takes 10 minutes to shoot back to the top.

The windows surrounding the 107th floor Observation Deck are too wide for the window-washing machine to cover. Three times a year, Roko and James wash the windows by hand. Each time, it takes them two weeks to finish.

21

**Roko works on the building's windows with a squeegee, a brush, and a sponge.**

Before they start cleaning, Roko and James each place a blue harness and bright yellow safety belts over their brown jump suits. Then, they step into the basket rig.

"These are my tools," Roko says, pointing at a squeegee, brush, sponge, and bucket filled with water.

Before he steps into the
basket, Roko secures
himself with a harness
and safety belts.

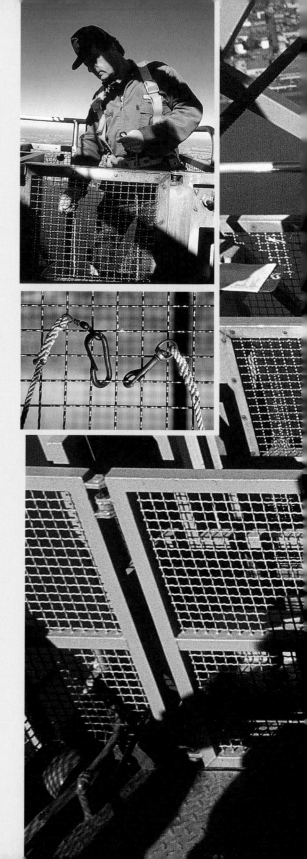

The washers fasten themselves into the rig. The brush and squeegee are also each attached to a small rope. At the other end of the rope is a clip, which connects to the wire mesh surrounding the cart. The clip prevents the items from falling to the ground if one of the tools slips out of Roko's hand.

"A penny can kill somebody if it's dropped from up here," Roko says. He's quick to add that a dropped brush would likely shatter "like a bomb" on the ground below.

24

**Roko and his partner
James enjoy the view
before beginning work.**

A worker on the roof stands ready to help if the washers should run into trouble.

26

As Roko and James work, another man on the roof oversees the controls. If the washers get into any danger, the man on the roof takes action.

Occasionally, a screw in one of the tracks will wear out. As the rig moves down the tower, the pressure can force a screw to pop out. If this happens, the rig's track will actually bend away from the building. If the cart starts to fall off the track, the washers ask the controls operator for help.

While every window washer is aware of the potential for danger, Roko spends little time worrying. "There are so many people here to help us," he says. "This is not really a dangerous job."

**Roko checks the window-washing machine's fuse box on the roof and calls downstairs to report what he saw.**

Most of the time, Roko is busy observing the changing city from his perch above the clouds. Recently, many new office buildings have sprung up nearby.

"Everything looks so different now," Roko says, pointing down at the island below. "When I started here, there was only dirt near the water. Now, with all these buildings, it's beautiful. I love it."

Roko works so high up that the weather is often different for him than on the street below.

Roko is so high in the air that the weather is often different for him than it is on the ground. Once, his supervisor called him on the walkie-talkie and asked, "What's it like up there?"

"It's snowing," Roko said.

His boss was surprised. "Down here, it's already turned to rain," he replied.

On another occasion, Roko was happily working in the sun. But it was raining on the sidewalk. The drops didn't hit Roko because he was washing windows above the clouds.

Even though Roko loves his job, he doesn't recommend that young people follow his path. "I was an immigrant, and this was the job I took," he says. "Kids today should try to do something different— they should study and get an education." Roko also thinks that his skills may not be needed much longer. "Ten years from now, all window washing will probably be done by a machine," he says. In the meantime, Roko will continue his work, enjoying the special view he has of the world from so high up in the sky.

**Roko enjoys his unique job high above the clouds in New York.**

# FURTHER READING

Brown, Richard. *A Kid's Guide to New York City*. San Diego: Harcourt Brace, 1988.

Cooper, J. *Skyscrapers*. Vero Beach, FL: Rourke, 1991.

Glassman, Bruce. *New York.*. Woodbridge, CT: Blackbirch, 1992.

Kerson, Adrian. *Terror in the Towers: Amazing Stories from the World Trade Center Disaster*. New York: Random, 1993.

Munro, Roxie. *The Inside-Outside Book of New York City*. New York: Putnam, 1985.

Wilcox, Charlotte. *A Skyscraper Story*. Minneapolis, MN: Carolrhoda Books, 1990.

# INDEX